The Answer to Bad Religion Is Not No Religion

LEADER'S GUIDE

A Guide to Good Religion for Seekers, Skeptics, and Believers

The Answer to Bad Religion Is Not No Religion

LEADER'S GUIDE

*A Guide to Good Religion
for Seekers, Skeptics, and Believers*

MARTIN THIELEN

WITH
JESSICA MILLER KELLEY

WESTMINSTER
JOHN KNOX PRESS
LOUISVILLE · KENTUCKY

First edition
Published by Westminster John Knox Press
Louisville, Kentucky

14 15 16 17 18 19 20 21 22 23 — 10 9 8 7 6 5 4 3 2 1

Book design by Drew Stevens
Cover design by designpoint.com

Library of Congress Cataloging-in-Publication Data

Thielen, Martin, 1956-
    The answer to bad religion is not no religion—leader's guide / Martin Thielen ; leader's guide by Jessica Miller Kelley. — First Edition.
        pages cm
    ISBN 978-0-664-25960-0 (alk. paper)
    1. Apologetics—Study and teaching. I. Kelley, Jessica Miller. II. Title.
    BT1107.T45 2014
    239--dc23
                                                                    2013041193

CONTENTS

INTRODUCTION

The increasing cultural skepticism surrounding Christianity, with its reputation for closed-mindedness and judgment, has resulted in many people abandoning religion. They've been turned off by hypocritical leaders, hate-filled bigots, aggressive evangelists, and smug believers convinced they know everyone's eternal fate. Many Christians want to stand up and shout, "That's not what our faith is about!" or "They don't speak for us!" but love and grace don't make for good television the way angry protestors do. To use commercial terms, the mainline "brand" of Christianity has not been near so well marketed as the more fundamentalist strain, for which many people now have little use or tolerance.

While this news is disheartening, and frustrating for many of us in the mainline church, we have a great opportunity to reach out to unchurched and dechurched people with a grace-filled, service-oriented, open-minded religion that can restore people's faith in, well, faith.

Many non-Christians today identify not as atheist or agnostic but as simply "unaffiliated," indicating their religion as "none." They've come to feel that religion is just not worth all the baggage it carries and that they are doing just fine without religion. Evangelism in this cultural climate is not so much about explaining beliefs to convince people intellectually but about demonstrating a faith that matters, showing people who are content without religion what "good religion" is all about.

This study inspires and equips mainline Christians to better articulate their Christian faith in a positive, passionate way, helping them to reach out to religiously unaffiliated neighbors, friends, and family members in a meaningful way.

Studying the Book Together

This leader's guide is intended to help your Sunday school class, Bible study, or small group explore and discuss *The Answer to Bad Religion Is Not No Religion*, by Martin Thielen, together.

The book discusses bad religion, no religion, and good religion in sequence over the course of the entire seventeen-chapter book—taking readers on a journey of spiritual consideration and development. To break the book's message down into manageable segments for group discussion and keep each session proactive, this study is organized around negative-positive pairings—characteristics of bad religion and their respective "answers" in good religion.

Each session of this study corresponds with several chapters in the book. Participants may read the corresponding chapters each week, or read the book cover to cover and simply review each week's chapters in advance of the group discussion.

Your church may also choose to explore these topics together in worship through a sermon series that will help members and visitors alike embrace a more positive, passionate faith. *The Answer to Bad Religion Is Not No Religion—Worship and Outreach Kit* equips leaders to craft sermons, plan worship, and promote the series to your community. The six weeks of worship and preaching outlined in the kit correspond to the six weekly themes discussed in this study.

WEEK 1

The Answer to Bad Religion Is Not No Religion, but Good Religion

This session introduces the overall message of the series, articulating in general terms the problem of bad religion in our culture, the common response of rejecting religion entirely, and the alternative response of embracing good religion, with the imperative for mainline Christians to boldly and visibly demonstrate this good religion to a skeptical world.

WEEK 2
The Answer to Judgment Is Love

This session juxtaposes judgment and condemnation with love of God and neighbor, practiced in compassion, tolerance, acceptance, and selfless service to others. While our judgments are selective and hypocritical, God's judgment is righteous and based on the way we love, not on the things we condemn.

WEEK 3
The Answer to Negativity Is Hope

This session emphasizes religion that is not simply against things, defining itself by what it is not (a temptation for both conservative and mainline churches), but that is affirming and proactive about what is good. Rather than lamenting the state of the world or the behavior of others, good religion is hopeful about the future.

Corresponds To

WEEK 4
The Answer to Arrogance Is Openness

This session confronts the arrogant spirit that convinces some religious people that they have all the answers, that they can and must be dogmatically certain in matters of belief and behavior. Good religion celebrates faith without certainty, keeping an open mind about new information, ideas, and situations.

Corresponds To

WEEK 5

The Answer to Division Is Community

This session addresses the temptation to conflate partisan politics or patriotism with one's religion, creating divisions between Americans of different parties and between all nations. Good religion promotes community—the interaction and mutual support of people within a congregation and across cultures.

Corresponds To

Chapter 4, "Bad Religion Participates in Partisan Politics and Excessive Nationalism"
Chapter 12, "Good Religion Builds Community"
Chapter 15, "Good Religion Practices Forgiveness"

WEEK 6

The Answer to Passivity Is Passion

This session juxtaposes nominal, lazy religion that may attend church or assent to certain beliefs without affecting the whole of one's heart and life. Good religion impacts our behavior and priorities seven days a week and shines forth in passionate faith that shares the gospel without even using words.

Corresponds To

Chapter 5, "Bad Religion Fosters Nominal Commitment to Christ and Church"

Chapter 8, "Good Religion Impacts the Way We Live"

Chapter 17, "Good Religion Practices Evangelism with Integrity"

Session Overview

Each session has three main sections, designed to draw participants in for deep discussion and send them out equipped for living and sharing a positive, confident faith.

— **Getting Started.** Begin each session with a brief summary of the week's topic and the chapters covered. This section includes an icebreaker to introduce the subject and get conversation rolling.

— **Reading and Responding.** The bulk of each session is spent discussing Scriptures and ideas presented in the book, examining beliefs and behaviors that contribute to bad religion and how we can better practice the good religion of Jesus.

— **Telling the Good Religion Story.** Each session closes with a discussion of how we can more effectively share good religion, both as individuals and as a church community, with those who have been turned off by bad religion.

Depending on the length of your group's time together, you can spend more or less time on each section. You may choose to read Scriptures and sections of the book aloud together or to let participants refer to them silently as needed to inform the conversation. The following time allotments are only a guide for planning and leading your study and can easily be adapted or ignored based on the flow and fruitfulness of your group's discussions. Always feel free to linger or move on to the next question as you sense topics resonating or not with your group.

	45-min. session	60-min. session	90-min. session
Getting Started	10 min.	15 min.	20 min.
Reading and Responding	25 min.	30 min.	45 min.
Telling the Good Religion Story	10 min.	15 min.	25 min.

Tips for the Group Leader

— Be aware of group dynamics and how much time is actually available for the study. Does your group tend to trickle in over the first fifteen minutes of class? Is it customary to end early to allow time for prayer concerns or socializing? If your group is being newly formed for this study, set a schedule and tone to enable a fruitful discussion and experience for all.

— Distribute copies of *The Answer to Bad Religion Is Not No Religion but Good Religion* at least a week before the first session, along with a list of the corresponding chapters to read prior to each session.

— As you prepare to lead each session, read the leader's guide for the week, the corresponding book chapters, and the Bible passages referenced. Make note of any additional sections or issues that you'd like to incorporate into the discussion.

— As each session begins, try to get a sense of how many people have read the chapters for the week. Do not shame those who have not read, but it is helpful to know how much background information you need to supply for the discussion to go smoothly.

— If any examples of bad (or good) religion have made headlines in your area recently, be prepared to discuss them in the context of the week's topic and readings, but do not let the discussion be derailed to focus solely on current events or solely on the negative.

— If a few group members seem to dominate the discussion, particularly with their own personal stories, be intentional about redirecting the conversation and specifically encouraging quieter persons to speak. Do not push anyone to speak who is not comfortable, but sometimes people have trouble breaking into a discussion with more assertive voices.

— Allow a few moments for participants to reflect and respond to questions before offering your perspective or pointing them to a particular verse of Scripture or page of the book.

WEEK 1

THE ANSWER TO BAD RELIGION IS NOT NO RELIGION, BUT GOOD RELIGION

This session introduces the overall message of the series, articulating in general terms the problem of bad religion in our culture, the common response of rejecting religion entirely, and the alternative response of embracing good religion, with the imperative for mainline Christians to boldly and visibly demonstrate this good religion to a skeptical world.

Examples of bad religion are all around us, from news of religiously motivated violence and bigotry to signs along the interstate claiming to know the status of everyone's soul. Bad religion like this turns many people away from Christian faith. A growing number of "new atheists" argue that since religion can be so toxic, we need to get rid of faith altogether. However, even if we wanted to, we are not going to get rid of religion, nor is it necessary to do so. The objections many people have to religion—reactions against toxic behavior, doctrines that insult their intelligence, and insufficient answers to life's problems—do not need to create the barrier they do between people and faith. Authentic Christianity does not arrogantly belittle others or require people to abandon either their brains or their questions.

When people reject Christianity based on bad examples and stereotypes, it is natural for us in the church to feel frustrated, misunderstood, maybe embarrassed. It is easy to get defensive, distancing ourselves from fellow believers who embrace beliefs or engage in behaviors we disavow, agreeing with critics of faith so completely that we forget to tell our own story.

This week, we assess the roots of bad religion and the temptation people feel to abandon faith together because of it. More importantly, we begin to think about how we can tell our story and show the world what good religion looks like: a religion of grace, not judgment; a religion of love, not hatred; a religion of open-mindedness, not intolerance; a religion of compassion, not legalism; a religion of humility, not arrogance. Just because some people practice bad religion doesn't mean we have to ditch religion altogether. The answer to bad religion is not no religion. Instead, the answer to bad religion is good religion.

Corresponds To

Introductions to parts 1, 2, and 3
Chapter 6, "No Religion Is Not Helpful"
Chapter 7, "No Religion Is Not Necessary"

Getting Started

Welcome participants to the first session of the study and introduce the overall concept. Make introductions if not all group members know one another, and make sure everyone has received a book. Begin the discussion with the following ice-breaker questions:

> What examples of bad religion have you seen lately? How do they make you feel about your faith and religion in general?

Reading and Responding

1. Read Luke 6:1–11, about when Jesus plucked grain and healed a man on the Sabbath.

a. What priorities do you see expressed by the characters in these stories? What do the Pharisees value? What do the disciples and the man with the withered hand value? What does Jesus value?

b. What similar interactions occur today, when people are more concerned with rules than with people's needs? Are you ever like the Pharisee in the story?

2. Read the Introduction to part 2 (pages 41–43). Do you agree that people seem "hardwired" to be religious? Is this evidence of the value of religion or, as some atheists say, a primitive response to fear and the unknown?

3. Read Psalm 10. What responses to human struggle are evident in this prayer? How does faith help the writer respond positively?

4. Reference, if necessary, the section "Benefits of Religion," from chapter 6 (pp. 47–49).

a. How would your life be different if you were not a religious person?

b. How would your community be different if there were no churches in it?

5. In chapter 7, Thielen identifies three major issues that turned his young friend off to Christianity: toxic attitudes and behaviors

from religious people, a literal reading of the Bible, and the problem of suffering.

a. Which of those factors are the most problematic, in your opinion? Do they ever make you consider abandoning religion altogether?

b. Why do you think stereotypes of arrogance, sexism, and ignorance persist, if the vast majority of Christians are not like that?

c. The problem of suffering can turn people not just away from Christianity but from God altogether. How can Christians play a role in shaping people's understanding of God when it comes to such complex and unanswerable questions?

6. What issues are most problematic for nonreligious people you know? Are they simply indifferent to religion or are they reacting against bad religion they've witnessed? Are their concerns mainly intellectual or emotional?

7. At the end of chapter 7, Thielen's skeptical young friend comes forward for Communion. If skeptical people do come to church for worship, how can the leaders and practices of the church help change their perceptions of religion?

Telling the Good Religion Story

Counteracting stereotypes (and real examples) of bad religion is a daunting task, one best handled positively and proactively. Discuss together how you can respond to nonreligious family and friends who raise the following objections and concerns about Christianity. If your group is comfortable with role-play, try to practice dialogue around the following topics:

Christians are all antigay, misogynistic, and superconservative. That's not me.

Scientific evidence proves that the world is billions of years old. Why should I think differently just because a really old book tells me to?

I can't believe in a God who would let little children be killed by a tornado.

My Muslim friend is the kindest, most honest, and most compassionate person I know. There's no way he's going to hell just because he isn't a Christian.

The Bible is full of errors and contradictions.

WEEK 2

⊂◦⊃

THE ANSWER
TO JUDGMENT IS LOVE

This session juxtaposes judgment and condemnation with love of God and neighbor, practiced in compassion, tolerance, acceptance, and selfless service to others. While our judgments are selective and hypocritical, God's judgment is righteous and based on the way we love, not on the things we condemn.

There's nothing wrong with having convictions about matters of belief and morality, but our convictions should never be an excuse to be hateful or violent or to self-righteously pass judgment when we have no right to judge. Jesus was harsh and clear with those he encountered who passed judgment on others, whether it was a woman caught in adultery, a corrupt tax collector, or Samaritans who worshiped God differently from Jews. No matter how much we disagree with someone—and no matter how much they may disagree with us—Jesus calls us to love and serve everyone with the same heart we would serve Jesus himself.

Jesus' emphasis was always on love. When Jesus was asked, "Of all the commandments, which is the most important?" he responded, "Love the Lord your God with all your heart, and with all your soul, and with all your mind, and with all your strength" (Mark 12:30). This isn't just emotional love—it's whole-body, whole-life love that demonstrates itself in active, self-sacrificial service.

We show love to our neighbors by feeding and caring for those in need, but that's also a prime way we show love to God. Yes, we express love to God in worship and prayer, but Jesus made it clear that when we serve others, we are serving God as well. In fact, the section of Matthew 25 where Jesus explains that is often called "the last judgment," as it says God will ultimately judge us by the love we show or don't show to others.

While our judgments of one another are selective and hypocritical, God's judgment is righteous and based on the way we love, not the things we condemn.

Corresponds To

Chapter 1, "Bad Religion Engages in Self-Righteous Judgment of Others"
Chapter 9, "Good Religion Prioritizes Love"
Chapter 10, "Good Religion Engages in Service"

Getting Started

Remind participants of last week's topic and the chapters being discussed this week. Introduce this week's subject with your own synopsis of the summary above. Begin the discussion with the following icebreaker questions:

> Who are you most tempted to pass judgment on? Why do you judge them?

Reading and Responding

1. Read Matthew 7:1–5. The metaphor of pointing out a speck in another's eye while ignoring the log in one's own eye illustrates how judgment is selective and hypocritical.

   a. What examples of "specks and logs"

have you witnessed among religious people or even in your own life? Are there specks you love to point out or logs that you love to ignore?

b. What do you think Jesus means by "with the judgment you make, you will be judged"?

2. Read Thielen's "clarification" in the third paragraph of chapter 1 (p. 4) and John 8:11, the end of the story about the woman caught in adultery.

a. How do we uphold our convictions and hold people accountable for wrongdoing without being judgmental? What about when the definition of "wrongdoing" is subjective?

b. If judgment is contrary to the example of Jesus, how do we emulate Jesus in his instruction to the woman not to sin again?

3. Read Luke 6:27–37, part of Jesus' "Sermon on the Plain."

a. Why does the admonition, "Do not judge," immediately follow instructions on loving those who hate and curse (and, presumably, judge) you?

b. How is loving an enemy different from loving a friend or family member? Does it require you to show your love in a different way?

4. Sadly, Christians are often more judgmental than non-Christians, and less loving. Knowing that all people are capable of showing great love, what makes a Christian's love unique? How should the example of Jesus shape the way we treat others?

5. Read the "family resemblance" story from chapter 9 (pp. 76–77). What would it mean to see every person we met — friends, enemies, strangers, "wrongdoers" — as children of God? What resemblance do we all have to God, regardless of religion?

6. Read Matthew 25:31–46, in which God separates those who actively cared for "the least of these" from those who did not.

   a. Do you read this passage as an indicator of God's criteria for salvation? If so, what would that mean about the importance of beliefs and religious identity?

   b. What does it mean for you that serving others is the same as serving Jesus?

7. Read the story of Jacoby in chapter 10 (pp. 80–83). Do you agree with Rabbi Isaac that it is harder to give to another person than it is to give to God? Why?

People naturally bond over shared negative feelings. This is the logic behind gossip among friends and the political adage, "The enemy of my enemy is my friend." Our relationships are—temporarily and superficially, at least—strengthened by criticizing and judging others.

"Did you see how Pat acted at the company picnic? He must have a drinking problem."

"What more can you expect from those kinds of people?"

But have you ever known someone who refused to engage in this kind of negative talk—someone who literally never said a bad word about anyone? Their kindness stands out!

What would it take for Christians to be known as people who never pass judgment and who love everyone? Discuss how we can work toward being those sorts of people individually and as a church. How can we show love to people whom Christians have traditionally judged?

WEEK 3

THE ANSWER
TO NEGATIVITY IS HOPE

This session emphasizes religion that is not simply against things, defining itself by what it is not (a temptation for both conservative and mainline churches), but that is affirming and proactive about what is good. Rather than lamenting the state of the world or the behavior of others, good religion is hopeful about the future.

We need to learn to identify and articulate our beliefs, values, and purpose in positive terms, not by condemning and distancing ourselves from those with whom we disagree. We must tell the world what we are for, not just what we are against.

Rather than lamenting the state of the world or condemning the behavior of others, good religion has a positive outlook, always being grateful for the good and hopeful that wrongs in the world can be made right. Religion, however, need not always be happy and easygoing. Pain and suffering need acknowledgment and response. Sin is real. But a constant negative and critical spirit is not the spirit of healthy faith. At heart, faith is about love, hope, joy, peace, gratitude, and wonder. Chronic negativism is an enemy to true faith, which sees what is good and what is possible and helps others to see it as well.

Gratitude is a first, crucial step, as we choose to recognize the good in any situation. The apostle Paul chose gratitude in spite of many negative circumstances—persecution, physical torture, conflict with other believers, shipwrecks, and imprisonment. In the midst of all these circumstances, good and bad, Paul wrote again and again about thankfulness and gratitude. To the Thessalonians, he wrote, "Give thanks in all circumstances; for this is God's will for you in Christ Jesus" (1 Thess. 5:18 NIV).

Good religion recognizes that good can always be found in any situation. Even if the good can't be seen at present, there is always hope for good in the future—hope that overpowers the temptation toward negativity or despair. Hope is at the heart of the Christian faith, rooted in the resurrection of Jesus Christ. That resurrection hope sees the possibility for good in every situation, giving thanks in all things and casting a vision for a more positive future.

Corresponds To

Chapter 2, "Bad Religion Expresses a Chronic Spirit of Negativity"

Chapter 11, "Good Religion Provides a Prophetic Voice"

Chapter 13, "Good Religion Is Hope Filled"

Chapter 16, "Good Religion Promotes Gratitude"

Getting Started

Remind participants of last week's topic and the chapters being discussed this week. Introduce this week's subject with your own synopsis of the summary above. Begin the discussion with the following icebreaker questions:

> Do you ever define yourself or your faith by what it is not, or what it is against? How does that description affect your attitudes

toward and relationships with people who embody the things you are so against?

Reading and Responding

1. Have you run into people in the church like the angry critics Thielen describes in chapter 2? What impact do they have on the church as a whole?

2. Jesus is described in several places as getting angry (Mark 3:5; John 2:15). What distinguishes righteous anger from chronic negativity?

3. Read Philippians 4:11–13 and 1 Thessalonians 5:18.

   a. What is Paul's secret to contentment? How does this help him resist the urge toward negativity?

   b. How do gratitude and hope lead to contentment?

4. Read the story of John Claypool in chapter 16 (p. 135). Remembering that the problem of suffering is one of the major barriers to faith for some people (chapter 7), how might an emphasis on gratitude

help skeptical people grow more open to good religion?

5. Read the story of Desmond Tutu at the beginning of chapter 11 (pp. 85–86).

   a. When we witness wrongdoing and suffering (apartheid, disease, human trafficking, etc.), how can we respond to despair with hope?

   b. What is the connection between hope and having a prophetic voice?

6. What does the word "prophet" mean to you? How can people in the church be prophets today?

7. Read 1 Corinthians 15:55–58. How does the resurrection of Jesus Christ give us hope in the face of troubles? How does it give us confidence to work for good and call others to do the same?

Telling the Good Religion Story

Thielen named consumerism and environmental irresponsibility as two issues on which Christians should speak out with a prophetic voice. What issues stir in you a righteous anger? How can you respond to those problems proactively, with a spirit of hope?

Think as a group about the places of negativity in your community. Where are there anger and hostility? Where do people seem hopeless about the possibility that things will ever get better? Do you see bad religion at work, casting blame for the community's problems? What could you do to demonstrate hope and a vision for a better future?

WEEK 4

THE ANSWER
TO ARROGANCE
IS OPENNESS

This session confronts the arrogant spirit that convinces some religious people that they have all the answers, that they can and must be dogmatically certain in matters of belief and behavior. Good religion celebrates faith without certainty, keeping an open mind about new information, ideas, and situations.

Uncertainty can make people uncomfortable. But absolute certainty is generally not possible; ambiguity is part of life. Unfortunately, a lot of Christians claim to have absolute certainty, closing their minds to any new or conflicting ideas, and they often come across as arrogant and become intolerant of anyone who disagrees with their rigid positions. Arrogant, intolerant religion is not the spirit of Jesus and is not a part of healthy faith. That's why Jesus taught his followers to reject arrogant religion and be humble in our approach to faith.

Good religion keeps an open mind. Acknowledging our limited understanding is not a sign of weak faith. As one wise believer once said, "The opposite of faith is not doubt but certainty." As Hebrews 11:1 says, faith is having confidence in something that is not seen or proven.

Being open-minded still allows us to have core convictions, values, beliefs, and practices. Christians obviously have some nonnegotiables, primarily around the life, death, and resurrection of Jesus Christ. But we think deeply about complex issues, using not just the words in Scripture but understandings and practices passed down in our religious traditions, our experiences of God and the world, and, yes, our own reasoning abilities.

Thinking deeply about God, our beliefs, and morals is a sign of faith, as our love for God draws us to learn and understand more and more, though we will never understand fully. As the apostle Paul said, "We see in a mirror, dimly" and "We know only in part," but he also said that God has given us the gifts of faith, hope, and love. And faith, hope, and love are more than enough to guide us through life.

Corresponds To

Chapter 3, "Bad Religion Breeds Arrogance, Intolerance, and Absolutism"
Chapter 14, "Good Religion Keeps an Open Mind"

Getting Started

Remind participants of last week's topic and the chapters being discussed this week. Introduce this week's subject with your own synopsis of the summary above. Begin the discussion with the following icebreaker questions:

> What things are you absolutely certain about? What makes these things knowable in such an absolute way?

Reading and Responding

1. Think about the statement, "The opposite of faith is not doubt, but certainty."

   a. Do you typically think of doubt as a negative, a lack of faith? How do you define doubt?

b. In what way is certainty the opposite of faith?

c. How comfortable are you with uncertainty?

2. Read Hebrews 11:1–3. What definition of faith is given here? How certain should we be of the "things not seen" in which we have faith?

3. Read 1 Corinthians 13:8–12, where Paul writes, "We know only in part. . . . We see in a mirror, dimly."

   a. What things do we in the church today seek to understand? How would it change the conversation to acknowledge that we see these issues through a hazy glass?

   b. Verses 8–12 are the lesser-known lines in Paul's famous "love chapter." Why do you think Paul made this observation in the middle of his oration about love?

4. Read the story of Brad Hirschfield in chapter 3 (p. 20). How does arrogance in one's beliefs lead to unloving actions? How do we know when the firmness of our beliefs is beginning to trump our commitment to love?

5. Closed-minded faith often creates false choices: Genesis 1 or science, a literal Bible or no Bible, absolute truth or no truth at all. Have you ever, even unintentionally, perpetuated this thinking when discussing faith with others? What does it mean to practice "theological modesty"?

6. Anti-intellectualism, or the opposition to scientific inquiry and the use of human reason, is a major barrier to Christianity for many people. Some would see faith as a matter of the heart and not of the mind. What does it mean to love God with your mind? In what way could intellectual inquiry represent a threat to faith?

7. In chapter 14 (pp. 119–20), Thielen uses the Wesleyan Quadrilateral to evaluate the question of female clergy. Try applying the four parts of the quadrilateral (Scripture, tradition, reason, and experience) to a question your church has wrestled with (e.g. homosexuality, abortion, infant baptism, electric guitars in worship, etc.).

   a. Did using this method result in a single, certain answer? Did everyone agree on that?

   b. How did this exercise challenge your convictions or your ability to practice theological modesty?

Telling the Good Religion Story

Bill Nye and even Pat Robertson have said that, given only all-or-nothing choices about faith, people will choose "none." Recent demographic research indicates this to be true, given the rise in people claiming no religious affiliation. How can your church demonstrate an openness to questions and the gray area between black-and-white options?

Brainstorm together ways that your church could seek out or provide opportunities for open dialogue about issues that matter.

WEEK 5

THE ANSWER
TO DIVISION
IS COMMUNITY

This session addresses the temptation to conflate partisan politics or patriotism with one's religion, creating divisions between Americans of different parties and between all nations. Good religion promotes community—the interaction and mutual support of people within a congregation and across cultures.

One of the great dangers of partisan religion is that it causes Christians to lose their prophetic perspective, both on the right and on the left. When the church is too closely identified with a political party or national identity, it can easily cloud our judgment as we put worldly agendas before our mission as Christians to love all people. And sadly, the costs of such mixed-up allegiances can be tragic, as was the case in Nazi Germany and apartheid South Africa. Therefore, Christians must resist partisan religion at all costs.

If our ultimate allegiance is to God, our identity as Christians trumps other identities we hold — our political party, our nationality, our race, our school, or our sports team affinity. When we allow these affiliations to trump our Christianity, we divide the body of Christ, damaging our churches and our witness to the world of what it means to have Christ as our Lord.

Maintaining unity of spirit and purpose in a church full of people who all have different opinions, preferences, affiliations, and priorities can be very difficult. The notion of "community" shouldn't be over-romanticized. It doesn't mean we always get along perfectly. It doesn't even mean that we all have to like one another. Do you get along perfectly and like everyone in your extended family? I doubt it. The biblical emphasis on loving, serving, and supporting one another does not automatically create some kind of idealistic, warm and fuzzy church where people never disagree or have conflict. Conflict between Christians, just like conflict between any people, is inevitable, but as Christians we are called to forgive one another and work together for the good of the world.

Corresponds To

Chapter 4, "Bad Religion Participates in Partisan Politics and Excessive Nationalism"
Chapter 12, "Good Religion Builds Community"
Chapter 15, "Good Religion Practices Forgiveness"

Getting Started

Remind participants of last week's topic and the chapters being discussed this week. Introduce this week's subject with your own synopsis of the summary above. Begin the discussion with the following icebreaker questions:

> Do you usually feel like you have more in common with non-Christians who share your political views or fellow Christians who do not? Why do you think that is?

Reading and Responding

1. Read Isaiah 40:15–17, 22–23, where the prophet extols the magnitude and majesty of God. What perspective does this

passage give on the priority we should give our political and national affiliations?

2. Read the story of Thielen's parishioner who considered himself "an American first and a Christian second" (chapter 4, pp. 27–28).

   a. What is the danger of this thinking?

   b. What role can or should national identity play in church? Many sanctuaries have American flags; some churches sing patriotic songs around national holidays. What do you think is appropriate?

3. Our political and religious beliefs do not exist in isolation from one another; many of us vote the way we do because of our religious convictions. In light of this,

   a. How can we ensure that our politics and our faith stay in proper relationship?

   b. What does it mean if faith leads Christians to different conclusions on a particular issue? How does this affect our relationships as Christians?

4. Read Ephesians 4:1–6, about maintaining unity in the church. What virtues should we all cultivate in order to live as one body of Christ?

5. Relationships are central to living as Christians, both for our own benefit and

growth and for the good of the world, as we can do more together than we can on our own.

    a. How have friendships and groups in your church helped you grow individually?

    b. How have groups and your church body as a whole made a difference in the world that individuals could not have made on their own?

6. Read Matthew 5:21–24, about anger and reconciliation. What do Jesus' words indicate about the significance of letting hostility and division linger in the body of Christ?

7. What divisions are there, large or small, in your church? How can you strengthen the unity of your community?

Telling the Good Religion Story

In the past few decades, religion and politics in America have become conflated to an extent that troubles even many Christians. Such partisan loyalties in the church have been especially troubling and off-putting to non-Christians. The alliance of churches with certain candidates and parties creates a barrier to faith when we send the message that to be Christian means voting a certain way.

Where do you see political divisions in your community? Even if it is not an election year, there are frequently protests and rallies near capitols and courthouses where both sides behave in rather "un-Christian" ways. What could your church do to help bridge these divisions, reconcile differences, and send a message that loving one another and the whole world as Christ did trumps our earthly allegiances?

WEEK 6

THE ANSWER
TO PASSIVITY IS PASSION

This session juxtaposes nominal, lazy religion that may attend church or assent to certain beliefs without affecting the whole of one's heart and life. Good religion impacts our behavior and priorities seven days a week and shines forth in passionate faith that shares the gospel without even using words.

American Christians don't do a very good job of living a positive, passionate faith consistently in all areas of life. Instead, we tend to be nominal and casual about our faith, especially those of us in mainline denominations. Several studies have revealed that less than 25 percent of U.S. church members bother to show up on any given Sunday, and the average American Christian gives less than 2 percent of his or her income to charity.

Of course, being a Christian involves far more than attending weekly worship. It also involves living a life of integrity, being a person of character, having Christian values, being compassionate, serving others, seeking justice, and affirming core beliefs about the life, death, and resurrection of Christ. Authentic faith needs to impact every part of our lives. But sadly, many American Christians exhibit little of this kind of commitment to Jesus Christ.

People can blame a variety of factors for the decline of the mainline church, but the heart of the matter may very well be lack of passion. If our faith doesn't seem to really matter to us or make a difference in our lives beyond our Sunday morning plans, why should anyone else join us?

Evangelism has become a scary word for many mainline churches because they have been turned off by pushy, manipulative, annoying evangelism tactics. But Christians and churches can do evangelism with integrity, and a lot of it comes down to living our faith boldly. One of the best ways we can witness to the Christian life is to live it! When we live like Christ—when we live lives of love, grace, compassion, integrity, service, and social justice—we testify that we are people of faith. People see our lives and think, "If this is what Christianity looks like, I'm interested."

Good religion is about so much more than avoiding the behaviors that turn people off to Christianity. We must live out the essentials of our faith with boldness, integrity, and passion. People not only tolerate that kind of religion but are eager to make it part of their own lives.

Corresponds To

Chapter 5, "Bad Religion Fosters Nominal Commitment to Christ and Church"

Chapter 8, "Good Religion Impacts the Way We Live"

Chapter 17, "Good Religion Practices Evangelism with Integrity"

Getting Started

Remind participants of last week's topic and the chapters being discussed this week. Introduce this week's subject with your own synopsis of the summary above. Begin the discussion with the following icebreaker questions:

> Where have you gotten lazy in practicing your faith? Worship attendance? Giving?

Serving others? Personal prayer and devotion?

Reading and Responding

1. Read the humorous "We Just Love Our Church" letter in chapter 5 (pp. 34–35). Can you identify with this situation? Should churches make regular attendance a clear expectation of membership, as do the Rotary Club and kids' sports leagues?

2. Read Revelation 3:15–16, a warning against lukewarm faith. What does it mean to be "hot" or "cold" in matters of religion? What is the danger of being lukewarm?

3. How would Christianity in America today be different if persecution were a real threat? What would it mean to be a Christian in that climate?

4. Read Matthew 5:13–16, about being salt and light.

   a. What are some practical examples of being salt and light in the world today?

   b. In what ways today do we hide our light under "bushel baskets"?

5. Read the section "Under the Cross of Christ" in chapter 8 (pp. 66–67). If every

aspect of our lives was different because of our commitment to Jesus, how would the following areas of your life be transformed?

— Calendar
— Family life
— Finances
— Bedroom
— Workplace
— Car
— Holidays

6. What is your reaction to the word "evangelism"? How would you describe evangelism at its worst and at its best?

7. Three ways to practice evangelism with integrity are life-style evangelism, relational evangelism, and invitational evangelism.

   a. Which of these are you most comfortable with? Which should you try to practice more frequently?

   b. Talking about our faith, even in the context of existing relationships, is intimidating for many people. What would you say if someone asked you "the reason for the hope you have" (1 Pet. 3:15 NIV)? Today, that question might sound like, "How can you be so calm when the world is such a mess?"

Telling the Good Religion Story

In Romans 10:14, Paul rhetorically asks how people will know the good news of Christ if no one tells them. People have heard a lot of bad news out of the mouths of Christians—news of judgment, division, and doom and gloom. The bringers of bad news shout loudly and get a lot of attention. How will people know that there is good, hopeful, loving, open-minded religion unless we share that good news boldly?

Discuss and commit to one another ways that you will live your faith more passionately going forward, in a way that will make people say, "If that's what Christianity is like, I'm interested."